DID ANYTHING GOOD COME OUT OF...

THE VIETNAM WAR?

PHILIP STEELE

WAYLAND

First published in Great Britain in 2015 by Wayland

Produced for Wayland by Tall Tree Ltd
Designers: Jonathan Vipond and Ed Simkins
Editors: Jon Richards and Joe Fullman

Dewey number: 959.7'043-dc23
ISBN 978 0 7502 9590 1

FSC

an imprint of Hachette Children's Group
Part of Hodder and Stoughton
Carmelite House
50 Victoria Embankment
London EC4Y 0DZ

An Hachette UK Company
www.hachette.co.uk
www.hachettechildrens.co.uk

Printed and bound in China

10 9 8 7 6 5 4 3 2 1

The publisher would like to thank the following for their kind permission to reproduce their photographs:

Key: (t) top; (c) centre; (b) bottom; (l) left; (r) right

The following images are public domain: Front Cover c br. Back Covr tl cb bl cr. Endpapers.
4–5b, 4–5c, 5cr, 6bl tr, 7c tr bl, 9cr bl, 10cl tr c, 10–11b, 11tr cr, 14–15c, 15cr b, 16–17t cr, 18c, 9tl b, 20cl, 20–21c, 21r, 22tl tr br, 25l, 26c, 27tl, 27br, 28bl, 28r, 29tr cr, 30cl b, 30–31b, 31tr, 32br, 32–33c, 33tr br, 34bl, 34–35c, 35tr bl, 36cl, 37br, 38–39c b, 42–43c, 43cr bl, 47br.

All other images istock.com unless otherwise indicated.
Front Cover bl Paul Goyette. Back Cover
5tl Icemanwcs, 12–13c Leena Krohn, 13bl Jean-Pierre Dalbéra, 24cl Dutch National Archives, 37tl Getty Images/CBS Photo Archive, 39tr Getty Images/Tim Boyle, 40l Dutch National Archives/Dijk, Hans van/Anefo, 41bl Pictorial Press Ltd/Alamy, 44tl Hu Totya.

Every attempt has been made to clear copyright. Should there be any inadvertent omission, please apply to the publisher for rectification.

CONTENTS

HELL AT KHE SANH

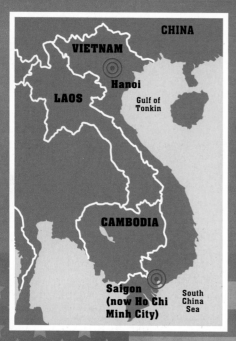

Vietnam lies on the Gulf of Tonkin and South China Sea, bordering China in the north and Laos and Cambodia to the west.

Khe Sanh is a village in Vietnam, just 10 km from the border with Laos. Back in 1968 there was a US army base at Khe Sanh with runways, tents, sandbags and concrete bunkers. The country was divided and the Vietnam War was at its height. To the north of Khe Sanh lay a 2 km-wide Demilitarised Zone (DMZ), which in theory separated the Communist Democratic Republic of Vietnam from the southern, US-backed Republic of Vietnam.

"NOW WE HAVE A PROBLEM IN MAKING OUR POWER CREDIBLE, AND VIETNAM IS THE PLACE."

US President John F Kennedy, 1961.

BULLETS AND BOMBS

For 77 days from 21 January 1968, Khe Sanh saw the worst fighting of the Vietnam War. About 6,000 US marines, as well as airmen and some South Vietnamese troops, were surrounded by 17,500 troops of the North Vietnamese army. Each side pounded the other with big guns, rockets and mortars. Huge explosions created big balls of orange fire, and the air was filled with the constant rat-a-tat of AK-47 assault rifles. However, the US airforce controlled the skies, and dropped over 90,000 tonnes of bombs on the enemy. US military chiefs even requested to use nuclear weapons, but this was turned down. In April, a relief force managed to get through to the base, reopening the road from the south.

A BREAKING STORM

How many North Vietnamese were killed at Khe Sanh? North Vietnamese sources say 2,469, while US estimates vary from 5,500 to 20,000. Perhaps 10,000 civilians of the local hill people, known as Degar or Montagnards, were also killed. The US forces lost 402 soldiers, and 2,249 wounded were airlifted from the base. That June, the US dismantled the Khe Sanh base and withdrew, still under fire. It had become clear to them early on that Khe Sanh was not the whole story. A massive new North Vietnamese offensive was underway.

Helicopters leave Khe Sanh base, carrying the last US soldiers and equipment with them.

"WAR, HUH, YEAH, WHAT IS IT GOOD FOR ? ABSOLUTELY NOTHING!"

'War', written by Norman Whitfield and Barrett Strong and performed by Edwin Starr for Motown – a hit song of 1970.

US soldiers based at Khe Sanh fire artillery at attacking North Vietnamese troops.

★ HOW COULD ANYTHING GOOD COME OUT OF A WAR? ★

In 1966, the first warnings were put on cigarette packets in the US. It said 'Caution: Cigarette Smoking May be Hazardous to Your Health.' A headline in *Newsweek* magazine proclaimed 'Being a Marine in Khe Sanh may be Hazardous to your Health'. This joke became popular graffiti at the camp, scrawled on buildings and jackets.

This book asks the question, 'Was the Vietnam War hazardous to health? Not only the health of the US and of Vietnam, but of the wider world?' The war split America. It divided generations and created opposition. Why was the war fought and what were the outcomes? Did any good come out of it?

THE CAUSES

How did the world's most powerful nation end up fighting a major war in a small, poverty-stricken country in Southeast Asia?

ROOT OF THE PROBLEM

In 1887, Vietnam was united with Laos and Cambodia as 'French Indochina'. Vietnamese nationalists began a struggle for independence. In 1919, during the Paris Peace Conference at the end of World War I, they asked to discuss the issue of independence with US President Woodrow Wilson, but were ignored.

When Germany defeated France in 1940 during World War II, a puppet French government was set up in France at Vichy. This Vichy government allowed the Japanese army to operate from Vietnam. The Japanese were attacked by the Viet Minh, an alliance of Vietnamese communists and nationalists led by Ho Chi Minh.

THE FIRST INDOCHINA WAR

By 1946, the Viet Minh controlled large areas of Vietnam, and declared a new independent state. The French met Ho Chi Minh for talks. They promised a deal, but then bombed the northern port of Haiphong and, in 1947, re-invaded Vietnam. The Viet Minh resisted, starting the First Indochina War.

The USA provided 80 per cent of the funding for France's war against the Viet Minh, setting up a Military and Advisory Group (MAAG) in the south in 1950. By 1954, 250,000 French troops were in Vietnam. However, they had underestimated the opposition. In 1954, the Viet Minh defeated the French army in an epic 56-day battle at Dien Bien Phu.

A French soldier followed by a US-supplied tank.

1859
French attack Saigon to protect Catholic missionaries and to gain control of resources.

1885
French gain control of the whole of Vietnam.

1919
Requests to discuss independence are ignored at the Paris Peace Conference.

FRANCE AGAINST THE VIET MINH
19 December 1946–1 August 1954

Republic of France/French Indochina (1946–1954), Republic of Vietnam (South Vietnam) (1949–1954), Kingdom of Cambodia (1953–1954), Kingdom of Laos (1953–1954).
Supported by the USA.
Total troops: c.400,000. Killed: c.94,000

Vietminh – League for the Independence of Vietnam (1946–1954),
Pathet Lao – Laotian fighters for independence (1946–1954),
Khmer Issarak – Cambodian fighters for independence (1946–1953)
Supported by: Soviet Union, People's Republic of China (from 1949)
Total troops: c.450,000. Killed: c.175,000–300,000

French troops open fire on Viet Minh soldiers.

WHAT FUTURE?

Ho Chi Minh, with Chinese support, led the communist Democratic Republic of Vietnam in the north while Bao Dai headed the rival Republic of Vietnam in the south, with US support. An international conference (left) held in Geneva in 1954 agreed that France would pull out and that Vietnam should be divided for the time being. The terms were not favourable to the North, but it was proposed that an all-Vietnam election for a united country should be held by 1956.

1947
France bombs the port of Haiphong and re-invades Vietnam.

1954
The First Indochina War ends with France agreeing to pull out of Vietnam.

THE SECOND INDOCHINA WAR

The election promised for 1956 by the Geneva Accord never took place, despite repeated calls from the North. Neither the South nor the USA had ever really accepted the proposal, which would probably have put Ho Chi Minh in power. Vietnam would not be reunited without a fight.

ALL-OUT WAR

On 2 August 1964, a report claimed that the USS *Maddox* had been attacked by North Vietnamese boats in the Gulf of Tonkin. On 4 August, another sea battle was reported. It is now known that in the first incident the USS *Maddox* opened fire first, and that the second battle never took place at all. However, the US Congress believed that the Gulf of Tonkin Incident had taken place and authorised all-out war.

The war escalated year by year. Forces from Australia and New Zealand were deployed and thousands of US Marines were shipped in through the port of Da Nang. In 1965, US planes carried out Operation Rolling Thunder, the intensive bombing of the North. Over three years, nearly a million tonnes of bombs were dropped, and maybe 52,000 civilians killed.

THE US INTERVENES

Republic of Vietnam (South Vietnam)

United States of America
Australia
New Zealand
Thailand
Khmer Republic (Cambodia)
Kingdom of Laos

Supported by: The Philippines, Taiwan, Canada, West Germany, United Kingdom, Spain, Iran

Total troops: c.1,830,000

Killed: c.480,000–807,000

1955
Start of the war as the USA takes over France's role as military adviser to South Vietnam.

1956
South Vietnam and the US reject an all-Vietnam election as proposed by the 1954 Geneva Accord.

1957
A communist rebellion breaks out across South Vietnam with US forces and local officials attacked.

1959
North Vietnamese fighters and weapons enter the South along the Ho Chi Minh Trail.

North Vietnamese soldiers carry weapons and supplies along the Ho Chi Minh Trail.

As early as 1957, armed opposition was growing in the South, and was aided by weapons and rebels from North Vietnam. Fighters were slipping into the South along the Ho Chi Minh Trail. This 2,400-km long route wound from the northern coast, down through the jungles of the western border, crossing into Laos and Cambodia and back again.

In 1960, a communist National Liberation Front was formed in South Vietnam with the aim of overthrowing the government. Its fighters were called the Viet Cong and they were supported and supplied by the North. In the meantime, the USA was pouring a lot of money into Saigon. By 1962, there were 12,000 US 'military advisers' in the South. In 1963, the Viet Cong defeated units of the South Vietnamese Army.

Democratic Republic of Vietnam (North Vietnam)

National Liberation Front/Viet Cong
Pathet Lao
(Laotian communist fighters)
Khmer Rouge
(Cambodian communist fighters)

Supported by: Soviet Union, People's Republic of China, Cuba, North Korea, Czechoslovakia, Bulgaria, East Germany

Total troops: c.461,000

Killed: 660,000 to 1.1 million

A US B-52 drops its bombs during Operation Rolling Thunder.

1960
Establishment of the National Liberation Front/Viet Cong.

1962
There are 12,000 US military advisors in South Vietnam.

1964
The 'Gulf of Tonkin incident'. US Congress authorises all-out war.

1965–1967
US troops increase from 200,000 to 500,000. US aircraft start Operation Rolling Thunder.

US sources claimed that the USS *Maddox* was attacked first in the Gulf of Tonkin incident.

9

AR LIKE WILDFIRE

US helicopter gunships

Name: **Lyndon Baines Johnson ('LBJ')**

Lived: **1908–1973**

Job: **President of the USA**

Johnson became US President after the assassination of John F Kennedy in 1963. He was a Democrat, a tough politician who championed civil rights and social reform. He greatly escalated the Vietnam War after the Gulf of Tonkin Incident, and ordered the secret bombing of Cambodia. He was followed as president by Richard Nixon in 1969, and retired to his ranch in Texas.

During the war, fighting could break out anywhere, even within the city limits of Saigon. US patrol boats took to the rivers, while helicopter gunships attacked enemy forces in the jungle. Other helicopters took troops into battle and then back to base.

US soldiers inspect a house on the hunt for suspected Viet Cong troops.

US Marines enter the ruins of the hamlet of Dai Do after several days' fighting during the Tet offensive.

HUNTING THE VIET CONG

US or South Vietnamese troops went through villages, fields and the jungle looking for the Viet Cong. In 1967, there was a big US offensive, but often the Viet Cong just seemed to vanish. It was discovered that they were using hidden networks of tunnels. Much of the war was fought with guerrilla tactics, but both the Viet Cong and the North Vietnamese Army also fought major battles, equipped with Soviet weapons.

South Vietnamese troops

1968
The Battle of Khe Sanh and the Tet Offensive. Massacre of My Lai. Battle of Hue.

1970
Peace talks begin in Paris.

THE TET OFFENSIVE

The Battle of Khe Sanh marked the opening of North Vietnam's Tet offensive. Tet is a celebration of the Vietnamese New Year. In 1968, it would not be remembered for its spring blossom, but for the attacks on a hundred or more towns and cities across the South (left), carried out by 84,000 Viet Cong and the North Vietnamese Army. The US generals were taken by surprise, but in the end Saigon was saved and the North and Viet Cong suffered massive casualties. However, the American public began to realise that any final victory would not come soon or easily.

LAOS

Major battles

CAMBODIA

VIETNAM

Clouds of black smoke rise over the city of Saigon during the Tet Offensive.

★ MASSACRE ★

For Vietnamese villagers, the war was a nightmare. Their crops lay ruined in the fields. In March 1968, US troops in the southern village of Son My murdered between 347 and 504 unarmed civilians, including children and babies. It became known as the My Lai massacre.

The city of Hue was virtually destroyed by fighting that year. When North Vietnamese troops and Viet Cong captured Hue, they executed hundreds of citizens. When Hue was recaptured, South Vietnamese troops also carried out killings.

1972
The Easter Offensive. North Vietnam attack on the South with 200,000 troops is repulsed.

1973
Ceasefire agreement, US troops pull out of Vietnam.

1975
North Vietnam invades South Vietnam, which surrenders.

END OF THE ROAD

US bombers were now flying across the border into Laos, attacking the Ho Chi Minh Trail and the communist rebels known as the Pathet Lao. US carpet bombing extended into Cambodia, where over 2,500 tonnes of bombs were dropped, 10 per cent of them untargeted.

NO MORE WAR?

In May 1969, the US assault on a mountain code-named Hill 937 (nicknamed 'Hamburger Hill') raised many questions. It succeeded, thanks to the extraordinary bravery of the US Airborne troops – but the hill was abandoned shortly afterwards. Had their sacrifice been in vain? Protests against the war became ever louder, both in the USA and around the world.

In Washington DC former US soldiers, or veterans, protest against the war in 1971.

PEACE TALKS

The year 1969 had seen the death of Ho Chi Minh, now replaced in the collective leadership by Le Duan, and in the USA, the inauguration of a new president, Richard Nixon. Peace talks now began in Paris. They would last over three years, as the war raged on. A ceasefire was finally signed in 1973 by all those engaged in fighting. It was never formerly approved, or ratified, by the US Senate, but US and Australian troops were withdrawn.

North Vietnam soon proved that it was determined to fight to the bitter end. In 1975, it invaded the South. President Nixon had promised in secret to defend Saigon with the air force if it came to the crunch – but by then he was no longer in office and the US Congress did not want to get involved. South Vietnam President Nguyen Van Thieu felt betrayed. There was panic in Saigon, and a mad scramble to escape by helicopter and ship. Within just 55 days South Vietnam had fallen and the Vietnam War was over. It was 30 April 1975.

> "IF, WHEN THE CHIPS ARE DOWN, THE WORLD'S MOST POWERFUL NATION, THE UNITED STATES OF AMERICA, ACTS LIKE A PITIFUL, HELPLESS GIANT, THE FORCES OF TOTALITARIANISM AND ANARCHY WILL THREATEN FREE NATIONS AND FREE INSTITUTIONS THROUGHOUT THE WORLD."
>
> US President Richard Nixon, 30 April 1970.

★ AFTER THE WAR ★

With its two halves reunited under a communist government, the new Socialist Republic of Vietnam faced huge problems. There was still anger and violence, resulting in persecution of former enemies. There was a devastated country to rebuild, creating huge economic problems. The Americans had serious problems, too. They needed to trace missing persons and prisoners of war left behind in Vietnam. Many had been tortured.

Many returning veterans had to come to terms with injuries or severe stress. Some had trouble adjusting to civilian life. Some felt bitter, blaming the generals, the politicians, the American public, the protesters or the media. Some became anti-war protesters themselves. Vietnam stayed a one-party state, but brought in economic reforms in 1986. The USA lifted its trade ban in 1994. Today, foreign tourists can visit the wartime tunnels of the Viet Cong and see captured military equipment (left).

POWER, BUT NO GLORY

The war in Vietnam was the final chapter in a long struggle for liberation and unity, fought by a people whose country had been invaded and colonised. Over the years, that struggle had been supported by many different people in Vietnam, including royalists and peasants, nationalists and communists. A similar clash of forces shaped the history of other Asian nations at that time, such as Malaya and Indonesia.

A UNITED, INDEPENDENT NATION?

Many US politicians sympathised with colonies fighting for freedom. After all, hadn't their own nation had to fight Great Britain for its independence in 1775? Ho Chi Minh himself had read out the US Declaration of Independence when he proclaimed Vietnamese independence in 1945.

In the end, the outcome of the Vietnam War was successful for those who wanted to see it united as a single independent nation. But to those who opposed communism, it was a failure, as the new Vietnam after 1975 was a communist state.

US President Eisenhower (left) meets South Vietnamese President Ngo Dinh Diem (right) in Washington DC in May 1957.

> "ONE OF THE WORLD'S RICHEST AREAS IS OPEN TO THE WINNER IN INDOCHINA. THAT'S BEHIND THE US CONCERN... TIN, RUBBER, RICE, KEY STRATEGIC MATERIALS ARE WHAT THIS WAR IS ALL ABOUT."
>
> *US News & World Report*, 4 April 1954.

14

RESOURCES AND TRADE

Were economics one reason for the Vietnam War? In 1954, US President Dwight D Eisenhower was very clear about the economic importance of the region to US interests. The USA was certainly eyeing up Vietnam's resources and trade opportunities, just as the French colonisers had before them. If the Vietnam War was indeed about economic benefit to the outside world, it failed to deliver. The region became unstable, and trade was held back for 50 years. By then the world's needs and the way its economy worked had moved on.

Today, Vietnam produces about 900,000 tonnes of salt each year.

Natural rubber was a key resource for Vietnam.

DEMOCRACY OR DICTATORSHIP?

President Eisenhower's biggest worry in 1954 was the threat of dictatorship opposing freedom and democracy. He was referring to communism, and recalling the brutal rule of Joseph Stalin in the Soviet Union between 1922 and 1952. In the coming years, the arguments about democracy were sometimes less clear. When it came to the proposal for an all-Vietnam election in 1956, it was Ho Chi Minh who was saying yes and South Vietnam and the USA who were saying no. The democratic case for US support of South Vietnam was undermined by one southern leader after another. South Vietnam's government was too often marked by corruption, coups, military rule, rigged elections and censorship.

VIETNAM WAR FIGURES

★ ★

Name: **Nguyen Cao Ky**
Lived: **1930–2011**
Job: **Prime Minister of Vietnam**

Nguyen Cao Ky commanded South Vietnam's air force before becoming prime minister in a dictatorial military government in 1965, which was led by Nguyen Van Thieu. He threatened to kill those who disagreed with him, and he angered both the public and the Americans. He declared that his hero was the German Nazi leader, Adolf Hitler. In 1971, he became vice-president of South Vietnam.

A mother with her baby votes during the South Vietnamese elections of 1967 which saw victory for Nguyen Van Thieu.

DOMINOES

To most US politicians, the biggest concern in the 1950s was the spread of communism. They believed that if one country became communist, a neighbouring state would follow and then another. US President Eisenhower said it would be like a row of dominoes falling down. This became known as the domino theory.

TOPPLING DOMINOES

Obviously, all sorts of political or cultural ideas can spread from one country to another very quickly, as can military takeovers and invasions. So why was communism singled out? Partly because of the early communists' emphasis on international revolution, partly because of the spread of communism into Central Europe after World War II, and also because of Chinese and Soviet intervention in the Korean War (1950–1953).

The aim of the Western powers in the Cold War was to stop this happening. When the Soviet Union did collapse in 1991, many people argued that this happened because successful military action by the West prevented many of those 'dominoes' from falling.

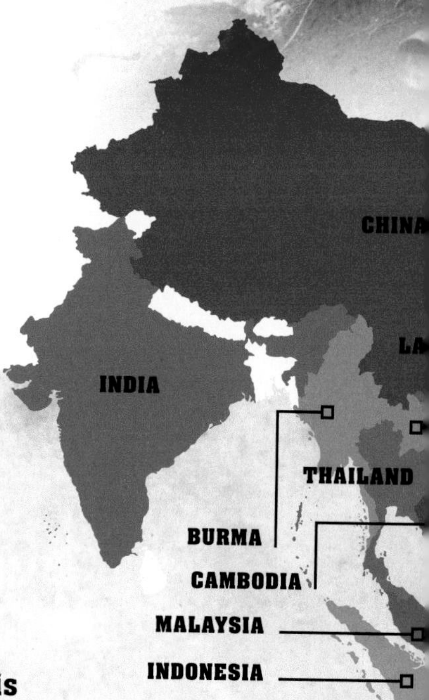

CHINA

INDIA

LA

THAILAND

BURMA

CAMBODIA

MALAYSIA

INDONESIA

The US was concerned that if one Asian country should fall to communism, the others would follow like a line of dominoes.

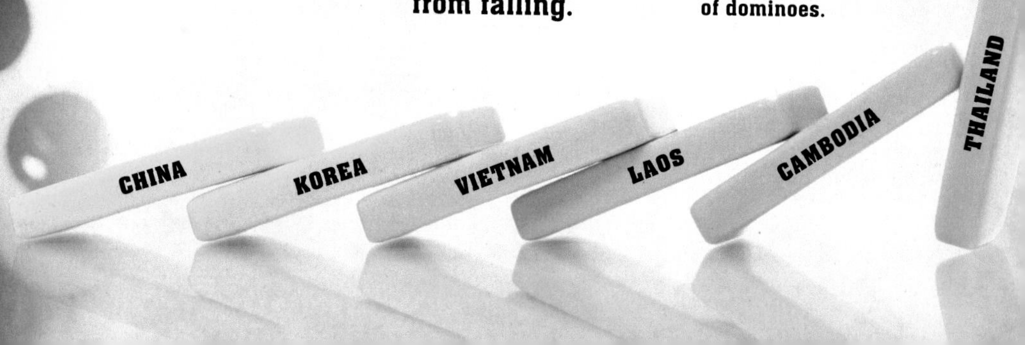

CHINA KOREA VIETNAM LAOS CAMBODIA THAILAND

REDS AND REALITY

So was the domino theory valid? Some historians believe that it was based on a simplified view of the world. In the early 1950s, US politicians encouraged a 'red scare', a fear and hatred of an all-powerful communist ('red') threat. But during the Vietnam War the communist world became rather more complicated. In the Soviet Union, Stalin had always disliked Ho Chi Minh, whom he dismissed as a nationalist. Had the USA forgotten that national liberation was a powerful driving force in Vietnam as well as communism?

MISJUDGEMENT

The USA may have over-estimated communist unity, too. From 1961 onwards the alliance between the two greatest communist powers, China and the Soviet Union, was beginning to fall apart. Ho Chi Minh was a communist with nationalist sympathies, but he had visited the USA as a young man and cooperated with Americans during World War II. Both China and the Soviet Union had persuaded Ho Chi Minh to accept the 1954 Geneva Accord. Might a diplomatic solution have prevented the war? There were times when it might have been possible – perhaps in 1919, in 1945, in 1956 or in 1964.

KOREA

VIETNAM

MALAYSIA

INDONESIA

BURMA

INDIA

POLITICAL OUTCOMES

Looking back at history, we cannot know the answers to these 'what ifs?'. We can look at the outcomes. The USA intervened in Vietnam, and it became communist. US attacks on the Pathet Lao (above) led to a communist government in Laos.

The bombing of Cambodia played into the hands of the communist fighters of the Khmer Rouge. This resulted in the horrific dictatorship of their leader, Pol Pot, and the death of 1 to 3 million people. None of the countries farther west became communist. In 1979, communist Vietnam even fought against China in a border war.

STALEMATE AT THE UN

The Vietnam War was one of the few occasions when the Cold War turned hot. Could it have been prevented or ended by the international community?

Secretary General of the UN, U Thant (on the left), with US President John F Kennedy at the UN Headquarters in New York City in 1961.

DIPLOMACY FAILS

In 1945, the League of Nations, which had failed to keep the peace in the years before World War II, was replaced by the United Nations (UN). A top committee of the great powers, called the Security Council, made the big decisions. Each member nation of the council had a veto – it could vote down any proposal that it disagreed with. At the height of the Cold War, that often meant that effective action was blocked, either by the Soviet Union or by the USA and its allies. As a result, US involvement in the Vietnam War was never even considered by the UN Security Council, as the US could simply block any vote.

U Thant, the Burmese Secretary-General of the United Nations from 1961 to 1971, tried to break this logjam. He didn't believe that North Vietnam posed a threat to the security of the West. In 1964, he proposed talks between the USA and North Vietnam and a return to the Geneva Accord of 1954, but this was rejected by the US and by South Vietnam.

★ VIETNAM WAR FIGURES ★

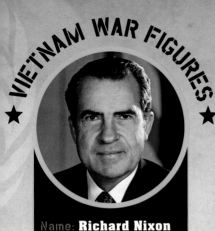

Name: **Richard Nixon**

Lived: **1913–1994**

Job: **President of the USA**

Richard Nixon was president of the USA from 1969 to 1974. At first, he increased US involvement in the Vietnam War, but eventually he was to oversee his country's withdrawal from the conflict in 1973. The Watergate scandal of the early 1970s saw him resign from office in 1974.

WAR AND THE LAW

Was the Vietnam war legal? Under Chapter 7 of the UN Charter (Articles 42 and 51), war is permitted if it 'maintains or restores international peace and security' or if it is carried out by a nation in self defence – or in support of another nation's self-defence. Some international law experts believe that the war was legal, but some disagree. In 1963, a UN Resolution did call for all states to respect the neutrality of Cambodia, but that was ignored by all sides.

The USA never issued a formal declaration of war against North Vietnam. In 1964, the US Congress passed the Gulf of Tonkin Resolution, a law allowing President Lyndon B Johnson to use military force in the region. As the truth about the Gulf of Tonkin Incident came out, this law was challenged and eventually repealed (cancelled) in 1971. Richard Nixon now relied on his powers as president under the US Constitution to wage war. In 1973, a new law was brought in to limit the powers of the US president, so that he or she could no longer go to war without the agreement of Congress.

US President Johnson (right) put forward the idea of a peace settlement to Soviet Premier Kosygin (left) that would have kept Vietnam as two countries.

HOW THE WORLD CHANGED

During the 1960s, communist China wasn't even a member of the United Nations. UN membership was restricted to the Nationalist Chinese government, which by then controlled only the island of Taiwan. This situation changed in 1971, when communist China was voted into the UN as a permanent member of the Security Council.

US President Richard Nixon visited China to meet Zhou Enlai (left) and to Moscow for talks with Leonid Brezhnev (below).

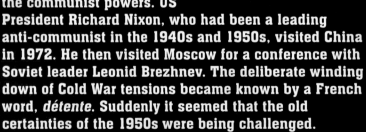

INTERNATIONAL RELATIONS

There began a thaw in the relations between the US and the communist powers. US President Richard Nixon, who had been a leading anti-communist in the 1940s and 1950s, visited China in 1972. He then visited Moscow for a conference with Soviet leader Leonid Brezhnev. The deliberate winding down of Cold War tensions became known by a French word, *détente*. Suddenly it seemed that the old certainties of the 1950s were being challenged.

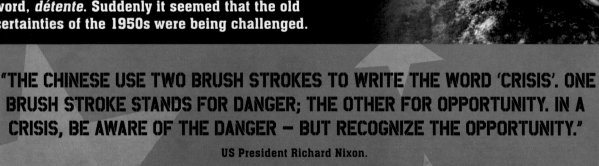

"THE CHINESE USE TWO BRUSH STROKES TO WRITE THE WORD 'CRISIS'. ONE BRUSH STROKE STANDS FOR DANGER; THE OTHER FOR OPPORTUNITY. IN A CRISIS, BE AWARE OF THE DANGER – BUT RECOGNIZE THE OPPORTUNITY."

US President Richard Nixon.

In the 21st century, US forces have been involved in major conflicts in Afghanistan (left) and Iraq (right).

AMERICA'S STANDING

US President John F Kennedy had believed that Vietnam was the place where America's political credibility would be tested. That testing would prove to be far more severe than he could have imagined. The My Lai massacre and the bombing of Cambodia shocked many people, losing much of the international goodwill that had marked Kennedy's presidency. It was now harder for the USA to claim the moral high ground. Even so, the USA remained the richest and most powerful country in the world.

For 20 years, memories of Vietnam haunted American policy makers. The USA became involved in many crises around the world, but generally avoided major wars until 1991.

THE 21ST CENTURY

In the 21st century, under President George W Bush, war spread across the Middle East. The Afghanistan War of 2001–2014 and the Iraq War of 2003–2011 brought back many of the experiences of Vietnam. Of course there were political differences, but many comparisons could be made. As a result, Bush's successor as US president, Barack Obama, took a more cautious approach to foreign wars.

Today, the question of intervention is made more complicated by the fact that the enemy may be guerrilla fighters, rather than large armies. When the two sides are made up of such different forces, it is called asymmetrical warfare, and it does recall the Vietnam War.

MEANWHILE, IN SOUTHEAST ASIA...

The newly united Vietnam spent years fighting and quarrelling with China. The dispute was about the border between the two countries. There were also armed clashes with the Khmer Rouge in Cambodia, which turned into a long war. Peace was not made until 1991. In 2007, Vietnam was admitted to the United Nations.

DOLLARS FOR WAR

During the evacuation of Saigon, US soldiers push a helicopter overboard to allow more helicopters filled with evacuees to land on the aircraft carrier.

We know that the human cost of the Vietnam War was horrific. The political cost was hard to measure, but it did damage the USA. But what about the economic cost?

MONEY MATTERS

The expense of US military action came in at around US$111 billion (now worth at least US$677 billion). Aid to South Vietnam cost another US$25 billion (worth about US$150 billion today). If one adds in related costs, such as caring for veterans, the cost soars. The cost of the war affected the progress of President Johnson's Great Society programme, brought in from 1965 onwards, which was tackling urgent social problems, such as racial injustice and poverty in the USA. It wasn't just a question of funding. The war was creating an ever wider political gulf between progressive politicians and conservatives, who became more hostile towards welfare programmes.

MILITARY EXPENDITURE

In 1961, the outgoing US President Dwight D Eisenhower warned about the danger of what he called a military-industrial complex. He was talking about the close links between the armed forces, the arms manufacturers, the government and the US Congress. The danger was that this 'club' of super-powerful corporations and individuals benefited from ongoing military conflict. It could easily become unaccountable to the people and encourage the wrong international alliances. Critics feared that the Vietnam War was being driven forwards in this way. This set-up still worries people today. World military spending in 2014 was US$1.76 trillion. The biggest spender by far in that year was the USA (US$610 billion) followed by China, Russia, Saudi Arabia and the UK.

The Pentagon, headquarters of the United States Department of Defense.

TOP 5 BIGGEST DEFENCE BUDGETS

The US is responsible for nearly 30 per cent of the total amount spent on weapons on the entire planet.

USA US$610

CHINA
US$216 BILLION

RUSSIA
US$84.5 BILLION

SAUDI ARABIA
US$80.8 BILLION

UK
US$60.5 BILLION

THE ECONOMY OF VIETNAM

The wartime economy of South Vietnam was based on the free market, but it depended on US aid. In both the North and South, bombing and fighting caused massive damage. The wartime North had a centrally planned, state-owned economy. Land reform on the Chinese communist model caused great hardship, as it had in China. The North received aid from China and the Soviet Union, but few imports could get into the country.

The problems facing Vietnam after 1975 were huge, as it needed rebuilding – and not just the cities, towns and villages. The population had been bitterly divided since World War II, and there were ongoing ethnic and religious differences. Two very different economic systems had to be brought into line. Southern industries were nationalised in 1980. Inflation was rising, so in 1986 there was a programme of economic reforms. This liberalisation was known as 'renovation' or *doi moi*. During the 1990s, the country was opened up to international investors.

The skyline of Ho Chi Minh City shows that Vietnam today has a flourishing economy.

SOCIAL CHANGE

During the Vietnam years, the USA and many other countries went through great social changes. When the US involvement started in the 1950s, society was very conservative. But the following years saw increasing concerns about nuclear weapons. It also saw the rise of the civil rights movement, demanding social justice for African Americans. One of that movement's most important leaders, Dr Martin Luther King Jr (right), passionately opposed the Vietnam War.

VIETNAM WAR FIGURES

Name: **Jane Fonda**

Lived: **1937–**

Job: **Actress**

Jane Fonda is a successful American actress. She became a critic of the Vietnam War and a supporter of Veterans Against the War. In 1972, she visited North Vietnam, where she was photographed next to an anti-aircraft gun. The US press called her unpatriotic and gave her the nickname 'Hanoi Jane'. Fonda has explained her actions many times since, but is still bitterly criticised in military circles.

A YOUTH REVOLUTION

This period saw the rise of an exciting new youth culture, spreading around the world. These young people challenged their parents' world through rebellion, dislike of authority, love of pleasure, freedom of expression, music, illegal drugs, care for the environment, internationalism and optimism about the future.

The Vietnam War came to represent the opposite of everything these people valued. They despised militarism. Some young men refused to serve in the armed forces. They burned their draft cards (the cards ordering them to report for military duty) as a protest, and escaped north into Canada, or overseas. Conscripts made up about 25 per cent of US combat troops. Seventy-five per cent were made up of poor, working class or black soldiers. Children from rich families found it easier to negotiate a deferment or an easier posting.

War protests grew larger. They were mostly non-violent in the early days, but became less so as the years went by. In May 1970, the National Guard shot dead four unarmed student protesters at Kent State University.

A US recruit has his head shaved after joining the army.

> "THIS WAR HAS ALREADY STRETCHED THE GENERATION GAP SO WIDE THAT IT THREATENS TO PULL THE COUNTRY APART."
>
> US Senator Frank Church, 1970.

THOSE WHO WENT TO WAR

Conservatives and traditionalists detested and feared these protesters. They thought they were immoral, decadent, unpatriotic, naive, dangerous, irreligious and communist. In a way, though, both sides wanted the best for their country's future, as they saw it. The anti-war protesters themselves belonged to another American tradition, of rebels, free thinkers and optimists.

Most young people did not burn their draft cards or protest. They cut their hair and put on a uniform and went off to do their duty. Even in the army, though, the youth culture began to make its mark, with irreverent humour, informality and rock'n'roll music.

A LASTING IMPACT

So many fought bravely. So many of them died or were wounded and shipped back home. Gradually, the horrors of the war became better understood in the USA. Opposition to the war spread through wider areas of society and came to include leading politicians. The tide was turning towards peace, although many conservatives wanted to fight to the bitter end. To this day, they defend the war as a fight for freedom.

The youth revolution raged for another decade, but came under attack during the 1980s and 1990s, a period when money-making and conservative values made a comeback. Even so, the 1960s still had aftershocks – and society was never quite the same again.

25

WOMEN AT WAR

World War I and World War II had helped bring about changes in the role of women in society, in the way they dressed and worked and voted. The new American feminists of the 1960s were often among those who opposed the war.

A US Navy nurse checks on an American soldier in a hospital in Da Nang, South Vietnam.

About 11,000 American women served in South Vietnam. Many of them were nurses. Others worked as doctors, clerks, air traffic controllers or in military intelligence. American Red Cross volunteers also helped soldiers keep in touch with home, assisted with any personal problems, and organised recreation for the troops. South Vietnamese women also served in army and medical units. Other women came to Vietnam from many parts of the world as observers – as journalists and photographers.

VIETNAM WOMEN'S UNION

In North Vietnam, the Vietnam Women's Union (VWU) had been founded as early as 1930. The Viet Minh constitution drawn up in 1949 gave women equal rights at work and in the home, and offered paid maternity leave. Traditional customs, such as forced marriage and child marriage, were banned by the communist government in 1959. Many more women now learned to read and write.

In 1967, with so many people involved in the war, at least 35 per cent of all jobs had to be given to women by law, and up to 70 per cent of jobs in teaching. Men remained in the most senior posts, though. A huge number of women served in the North Vietnam Army and with the Viet Cong. They were in combat units and also worked as guides, porters, radio operators and medics. Officially, women's rights were still a priority after the war, but after the economic reforms of 1986, little further progress was made. However, the VWU still has 13 million members.

During the war, many Vietnamese women were arrested by US and South Vietnamese soldiers on suspicion that they were part of the Viet Cong.

★ESCAPING DANGER★

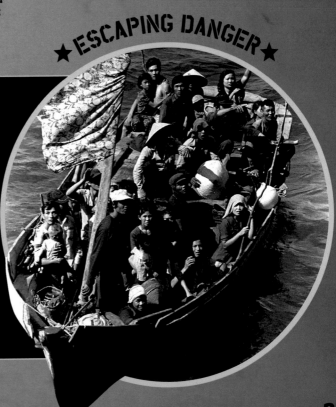

For men, women and children on all sides, the two Indochina wars caused hunger, sorrow, misery and death. There were great movements of people as political change and fighting forced them from their homes. US troops often destroyed crops in the fields if they thought they were being used to feed the Viet Cong, so rural villagers poured into Saigon. The city population in the South tripled between 1958 and 1971.

At the end of the war, many Vietnamese who had worked with the Southern government or the US army fled the country to the USA. During the 1970s, further wars, as well as economic and political reforms, caused many Vietnamese to flee to other Southeast Asian countries. In the late 1970s and 80s, there was a surge in refugees fleeing Vietnam by boat to Australia, Thailand or Hong Kong. These boat people faced dangerous sea crossings and attacks by pirates.

SAVING LIVES

Wartime emergencies often result in the development of new medical treatments or medicines which save lives in future wars or help society as a whole.

★EMERGENCY TREATMENTS

In Vietnam, paramedics learned to carry out major life-saving procedures before the wounded even reached a field hospital. These might include cutting an emergency airway to allow the victim to breathe, using a needle to relieve air pressure in the lungs, or shock resuscitation. These techniques became the model for today's pre-hospital emergency medical systems.

A US medic gives first aid treatment to a wounded marine during the battle for Hue City in 1967.

★ MEDICAL TRANSPORT

During the Vietnam War the helicopter was an important form of transport for warfare and for medical assistance. The key for getting wounded soldiers back to base was evacuation by helicopter, often under enemy fire – a method developed during the Korean War. This process was called dust-off. In dense jungle, it might involve winching up the casualty by cable.

With improved pick-up times and better radio contacts, flying ambulances and hospital ships saved many lives before the casualties were sent back home. It has now become normal in many parts of the world for helicopters to evacuate the injured from road traffic accidents, inner city crises or natural disasters, and many hospital trauma units have their own helipads.

The Bell UH1 Iroquois, or 'Huey', was used both to carry soldiers into battle and to carry the wounded back to field hospitals.

★ TREATMENT AT HOME

After first aid and surgery, wounded soldiers were flown back to the USA to receive further treatment in special military hospitals. Work with Vietnam War veterans greatly increased our understanding of the terrible stress suffered by many soldiers after combat or some other terrifying experience. It can cause nightmares, flashbacks, shaking and extreme anxiety. In World War I it was called 'shell shock', and in World War II 'combat fatigue'. US psychiatrists carrying out research adopted the term PTSD (post-traumatic stress disorder) in 1980. PTSD is suffered by one in three people who have undergone extreme shocks, such as terrorist attacks, assault or life-threatening accidents.

American football star Wendell Hayes visits recovering wounded soldiers at an army medical centre in 1972.

★ AMAZING GLUE ★

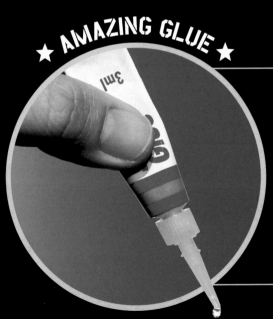

Two US soldiers carry a wounded colleague towards a helicopter (left). Quick evacuation of the wounded from the battlefield was essential to prevent further complications and infection.

Superglues were first developed by Kodak in 1959. Their proper scientific name is cyanoacrylate adhesives. Soon researchers were looking into possible medical uses and trials were carried out in Vietnam in 1966. It was found that in spray form these glues could seal up a chest wound or other serious injury, stemming the loss of blood. After more trials, surgical glues were approved for civilian use in the USA in 1998. They are now used in dentistry, surgery and home first-aid.

NEW TECHNOLOGIES

War often brings about scientific discoveries or new technologies. Tragically many of these are simply new or better ways of killing people, so are hardly great advances for humanity. However, other innovations do save lives, or have useful spin-offs in other areas.

★ NIGHT VISION

Night vision devices (NVDs) were first developed in World War II, but greatly improved in the Vietnam War. These versions could operate in moonlight or even just starlight. They captured the very small amount of light reflected from an object and boosted it a thousand times. NVDs can be used as scopes on weapons (left) or fitted into goggles. They can be used in surveillance cameras or mounted in helicopters. As well as having military uses, NVDs are often used today for security and law enforcement, observation of wildlife, and navigation.

★ LASER GUIDED BOMBS

The Vietnam War also saw the development of laser-guided bombs (LGBs). Electronic technology was used to direct them towards a light source, so the target first needed to be 'lit up'. In 1972, it was LGBs that finally managed to destroy the Thanh Hoa Bridge on the Ma River, which US aircraft had been targeting in vain since 1965. LGBs were the ancestors of the so-called smart bombs (precision-guided munitions) of the 1990s. Laser devices had been invented in 1960 and also came to be used in many non-military applications, such as surgery, printing, scanning, industrial manufacture and lighting.

Reconnaissance photograph of the Thanh Hoa Bridge after it had been destroyed.

M-16 rifle

AK-47 rifle

★ COMBAT WEAPONS

The various troops fighting in Vietnam, from the Australians and New Zealanders to the Viet Cong, used a wide range of weapons. Many of these were modified and improved during the course of the war. North Vietnamese troops were soon equipped with the latest Soviet or Chinese weaponry, including AK-47 rifles, DP 7.62mm light machine guns and the SA-7 Grail portable missile launcher. US troops fired M-60 machine guns and M-16 rifles, which were specially adapted for use in jungles, swamps and fields.

> "... IF MY RIFLE CLAIMED PEOPLE'S LIVES, THEN CAN IT BE THAT I... WAS TO BLAME FOR THEIR DEATHS?... THE LONGER I LIVE, THE MORE I WONDER WHY THE LORD ALLOWED MAN TO HAVE THE DEVILISH DESIRES OF ENVY, GREED AND AGGRESSION."
>
> Mikhail Kalashnikov, Russian designer of the AK-47 assault rifle, in 2013.

★ MISSILES

In the air, new missiles could home in on a source of radio waves, such as an enemy radar or air defence system. The US Navy first used the AGM-45 Shrike, an early anti-radiation missile, in Vietnam in 1965. By 1968, there was a much more efficient but more expensive missile in service, the AGM-78 Standard.

A US Marines jet launches an AGM-45 Shrike missile.

31

FIRE FROM HELL

Many of the technological developments have raised moral concerns over their use. These include powerful explosives, massive aircraft used to carpet bomb huge areas and pilotless drones which are used to attack targets beyond the war zone.

★ AIRCRAFT DESIGN

Many new aircraft designs and modifications were brought in for the Vietnam War. The standard helicopter of the conflict was the Bell UH-1 Iroquois, nicknamed the 'Huey'. It had originally been designed for medical evacuations, but a new model, the UH-1E, was ready for military action in 1964. It was now all-aluminium, with a new rotor brake and a rescue hoist on the roof. The huge Boeing B-52 Stratofortress bombers were also adapted during the Vietnam War, with extra racks or big 'bellies' for carpet bombing. Lockheed U2 'spy planes', a real symbol of the Cold War, were packed with surveillance equipment and adapted to fly over North Vietnam at an altitude of 20 km

A B-52 bomber can carry more than 30 tonnes of weapons and is still in service today

★ NAPALM

The Vietnam War saw a big rise in the use of a horrific weapon called Napalm B. This is a mixture of chemicals that sticks to the skin, burning at temperatures of up to 1,200°C. The USA dropped over 350,000 tones of Napalm B bombs in Vietnam, not only to destroy enemy positions but also to terrorise the enemy.

The use of Napalm B against civilians was banned by a UN Convention in 1980. The USA finally signed up to the agreement in 2009.

Exploding napalm can generate temperatures of up to 1,200°C, burning anything in the area.

Napalm was also used in flame throwers, such as the one fitted to this US river boat in Vietnam.

★ THE FIRST DRONES

Unmanned aerial vehicles (UAVs) were first widely used in the Vietnam War. They were remote-controlled aircraft with no pilot. One thousand AQM-34 Ryan Firebees (right) carried out more than 34,000 surveillance missions in Vietnam. These were the ancestors of today's drones. Modern drones can carry out many useful surveillance jobs. They can monitor radioactive areas without risking lives, or survey damage in an earthquake zones. However, they are often used as attack weapons outside war zones. This raises important questions of morality. Does remote murder become little more than a computer game?

CLEARING THE JUNGLE

A US helicopter sprays defoliants over the Vietnamese jungle in 1969.

Much of the Vietnam War was fought in jungles. About 45 per cent of Vietnam is forested, about 40 per cent of Cambodia and 68 per cent of Laos. This helped local guerrilla fighters, who knew every forest track. It made it very difficult for the US to track military movements and routes beneath the treetops.

★ 'ECO' WARFARE

To clear large areas of forest, the Americans used aircraft to spray defoliants. These chemicals stripped the trees of their leaves. During Operations Trail Dust and Ranch Hand, about 10 per cent of Vietnam was sprayed. Most of that was forested land, but also fields were sprayed to destroy crops. The two sprays were known as Agent Purple and Agent Orange.

They were said to be harmless to humans. But in reality, Agent Orange contained powerful toxins that poisoned the soil and remained in the food chain. Wildlife declined and many babies were born deformed. Since 2005, US agencies have been working with Vietnam's government to clear up the worst affected areas and any remaining stores (left).

★ JUNGLE TRACTOR

The Rome plow was a big, armoured bulldozer (right) used by the US army to clear the forest around bases or roads, so that the Viet Cong had no cover if they attacked. It was useful over limited areas, but could not clear large areas for aerial surveillance.

> "YES, THERE IS A STORY ABOUT AGENT ORANGE, AND WE KNEW THAT IT HARMED OUR TROOPS AND WE KNEW HOW LONG IT WAS TO GET THE MEDICAL COMMUNITY TO ACCEPT THAT, THE MILITARY TO ACCEPT IT, THE VA [US DEPARTMENT OF VETERAN AFFAIRS] TO ACCEPT IT."
>
> US politician, Christopher Shays.

★ FROM VIETNAM TO THE INTERNET

Perhaps the most important new technology in the Vietnam War was electronic. US Defense Secretary Robert McNamara (below left) was the first to use mainframe computers to analyse statistics about the war and use them to work out strategy. The data collection was not that reliable, but this was the road to the future.

A large mainframe computer from the period stored information on huge reels of magnetic tape.

At this time, the Defense Department became interested in communications and how to link up computers. It funded the Advanced Research Projects Network (ARPANET). ARPANET sent computer scientist Robert Taylor to set up a centre in Saigon. The aim was to coordinate computer reports sent to Washington. ARPANET sent its first message in 1969. Its technology would later form the basis of the internet.

MEDIA AND THE ARTS

During the 1960s, the US communications media were in the spotlight. Advertising, psychology, politics and new technology were coming together as never before. There was great public interest in the performance of presidential candidates on television. It was always clear that the media was going to play a big part in the Vietnam War.

NEWS AND CENSORSHIP

Afterwards, many politicians and generals blamed the media for undermining the war effort through negative reporting, and so 'losing the war'. Examining the newspaper and television coverage of that time does not really back up that theory. Although there was little censorship, newspaper and television bosses mostly made sure that their reporters and presenters toed the line.

In 1971, when opposition to the war was at its height, journalists did cause political earthquakes. *The New York Times* published parts of official US Defense documents. These Pentagon Papers revealed how US governments had covered up major escalations of the war.

In 1972, *The Washington Post* uncovered illegal activities by President Nixon's staff, who had broken into their opponents' offices. Nixon himself had lied and tried to cover up the crime. This was the Watergate Scandal. In 1974, Nixon was forced from office. As a result, South Vietnam no longer had its strongest international supporter. With US aid already reduced, the South was questioning how long it could survive.

The stream of violent images from the war changed many people's attitude to the conflict.

"IT'S THE FIRST WAR WE'VE EVER FOUGHT ON THE TELEVISION SCREEN AND THE FIRST WAR THAT OUR COUNTRY EVER FOUGHT WHERE THE MEDIA HAD FULL REIGN."

US General William Westmoreland.

"NO EVENT IN AMERICAN HISTORY IS MORE MISUNDERSTOOD THAN THE VIETNAM WAR. IT WAS MISREPORTED THEN, AND IT IS MISREMEMBERED NOW."

Richard Nixon, *New York Times*, 1985.

US reporter Richard Threlkeld interviews an American commander during a news report in 1969.

TV AND PHOTOGRAPHERS

The Vietnam War was the first war in which television ownership was widespread. Reports from the war were beamed into the sitting rooms of America, night after night. The images were real and immediate, and stripped away any of the romance or glory traditionally associated with battle. Few horrific images were shown, but relentless coverage, year after year, did have its effect.

The war did continue one tradition, that of the great photo-journalists who had recorded the Spanish Civil War in the 1930s and World War II in the 1940s. Powerful photographs, many in black and white, captured the ordeal of the troops on both sides, the suffering of the Vietnamese people and the horrors of war.

A US soldier reads *Stars and Stripes*, the newspaper of the armed forces.

Journalists and photographers were given free access to the battlefields by US forces. In later wars, that freedom would be more restricted, but it is those Vietnam photographs which tell the true nature of war, and leave one to respect those who had to cope with it.

37

ART OF THE WAR

In North Vietnam, artists recorded the wartime lives of villagers, farmers and soldiers in realistic but expressive styles, using pen and ink, pencil or water colour, often on whatever scraps of paper came to hand. Many were talented art students who were sent to the jungle trails and villages to record what they saw. Propaganda posters were produced too, often using more subtle and individual designs than in the Soviet or Chinese communist tradition.

Crowds gather in front of the stage at the opening of the Woodstock festival in 1969.

★POP FOR PEACE OR PATRIOTS

Popular music was the most powerful art form of the war. Some songs were satirical or angry, some were poetic or philosophical, some dealt with the plight of veterans, some longed for peace. The Woodstock Festival held in upstate New York in August 1969 became a high point in the movement for peace. Many of the biggest pop stars of the day were anti-war, from John Lennon and Neil Young to Janis Joplin and Joni Mitchell (right). The pro-war public also had their songs. 'The Ballad of the Green Berets', a patriotic song about a soldier killed by the Viet Cong, reached No 1 in the USA in 1966.

★STARS, STRIPES AND BULLETS

In the National Veterans Art Museum in Chicago, the entrance hall exhibits a sobering installation of dog tags (identity discs, left) representing US soldiers who died in Vietnam. The Vietnam War coincided in America with a period of experimental art styles, with abstract designs, Pop art and conceptual art all vying to shock the public. Many US artists were opposed to the war and featured images of bombers and death in their work. The artist Jasper Johns portrayed the American flag in black, orange and jungle green, with a bullet hole in the centre.
....

The sculpture is made from 58,226 dog tags and hangs in the entrance to the National Veterans Art Museum in Chicago.

"AND I DREAMED I SAW THE BOMBERS RIDING SHOTGUN IN THE SKY AND THEY WERE TURNING INTO BUTTERFLIES ABOVE OUR NATION."

'Woodstock' by Joni Mitchell, 1970.

★RED MUSIC AND SAIGON CLASSICS

In North Vietnam, the songs of the war were revolutionary anthems, remembered as *nhac do* ('red music'). South Vietnamese singers explored the war, the fall of Saigon and fleeing abroad, and their music is still remembered and played.

WRITERS, FACTS AND FICTION

Writers became interested in Vietnam early on. In 1955, the English author Graham Greene, who had been a newspaper correspondent in Saigon, wrote a novel called *The Quiet American*. The book describes an American agent during the First Indochina War. The book was made into a film in 1958 and again in 2002.

★ LEADING WRITERS

Many of the world's leading writers and thinkers opposed the Vietnam War, including Bertrand Russell and Jean-Paul Sartre. In the USA, a group called 'American Writers against the Vietnam War' was set up in 1965 and included the poets Robert Bly, Robert Lowell and Allen Ginsberg (left). Norman Mailer's *Armies of the Night* dealt with a 1967 protest in Washington DC, at which he was arrested. Michael Herr's *Dispatches* (1977) was part of what became known as 'the new journalism', because of its raw, energetic and often shocking account of the war as seen first-hand.

"I CAN'T SAY WHAT MADE ME FALL IN LOVE WITH VIETNAM... THEY SAY WHATEVER YOU'RE LOOKING FOR, YOU WILL FIND HERE. THEY SAY YOU COME TO VIETNAM AND YOU UNDERSTAND A LOT IN A FEW MINUTES."

The Quiet American, Graham Greene, 1955.

> **"I KEEP THINKING OF ALL THOSE KIDS WHO GOT WIPED OUT BY 17 YEARS OF WAR MOVIES BEFORE COMING TO VIETNAM AND GETTING WIPED OUT FOR GOOD."**
>
> *Dispatches*, by Michael Herr, 1977.

★ VIETNAM ON SCREEN

To later generations, the Vietnam War is mostly known through the cinema. The sheer number of films made in the USA and elsewhere in the world reveals the ongoing fascination with Vietnam. It includes gung-ho traditional war films, over-the-top action movies, psychological thrillers, comedies and anti-war films.

The Green Berets (1968) was a patriotic tribute by John Wayne to US Special Forces. Many films dealt with the return of veterans, from the action movies of the *Rambo* series (1982–2008) to *The Deer Hunter* (1978), a serious look at the effects of war on those who take part, starring Robert de Niro. *Apocalypse Now* (1979), directed by Francis Ford Coppola, is the story of a Special Forces officer sent upriver to track down a mysterious colonel who has gone absent to create a world of his own.

Many Vietnam films bore little relationship to reality, but director Oliver Stone was himself a Vietnam veteran. He made three Vietnam films – *Platoon* (1986), *Born on the Fourth of July* (1989) and *Heaven and Earth* (1993). Stanley Kubrick's *Full Metal Jacket* (1987) examines the effect of the military way of thinking on the individual, from boot camp to the Tet Offensive. *Good Morning, Vietnam* (1987) is a comedy starring Robin Williams as a DJ in Vietnam with the Armed Forces Radio Service.

Oliver Stone, director of several films dealing with the Vietnam War and its effects, including *Platoon* and *Born on the Fourth of July*.

In *Apocalypse Now*, the mysterious colonel leads this band of jungle fighters.

41

THE BIG QUESTIONS

How was it that the USA, the most powerful nation in the world, did not achieve its aims in Vietnam? The US forces and their allies had the most advanced weapons ever known and their highly trained troops rarely lost a battle on the ground.

WHO WAS TO BLAME?

So was it the fault of the politicians, or the generals? Had they become too sure of their own power and underestimated the enemy? Was it the media or the anti-war protesters turning people's heads and running down public morale? Was it surprising that young people at the time had their own ideas about the future? Was this just the wrong war at the wrong time?

Even with all its advanced equipment such as these tanks, the US army could not defeat the communist forces.

'ONE, TWO, THREE, WHAT ARE WE FIGHTING FOR?'

The Americans were fighting chiefly because of a political idea – the domino theory. Did people understand what that was about, or feel strongly enough about it to fight in a war? There was a popular satirical song in 1967, by Country Joe and the Fish. Its chorus began: 'And it's one, two, three, What are we fighting for? Don't ask me, I don't give a damn. Next stop is Vietnam.'

Of course, the North Vietnamese Army and the Viet Cong were also fighting for a political idea – communism. However, they were also defending their homes and the landscape they grew up in from a foreign invader. In any conflict, that may in the end count for more than anything else. The US troops could return home, but the people of Vietnam had nowhere else to go. Perhaps this fact

"TO JAW-JAW IS BETTER THAN TO WAR-WAR."

British Prime Minister Sir Winston Churchill writing in *The New York Times*, 27 June 1954. Churchill opposed US involvement in Vietnam.

★ HEARTS AND MINDS ★

Armies know they always have to win over the 'hearts and minds' of local people to be successful, but that was no easy task in Vietnam. Any villager they spoke to might turn out to be a Viet Cong fighter. In their fortified army bases, how could the Americans really get to know and understand their enemies, or even their allies?

A Viet Cong soldier stands beneath the flag of North Vietnam.

MORAL DILEMMAS

The big moral questions about the Vietnam War have applied to warfare throughout history. Was this in principle a just war? Can any war be just? What do we mean by patriotism? Were people who refused to fight the war on moral grounds justified in their action? In a democracy, are people bound to serve a government that has been elected by a majority? Or do they have individual rights of conscience? There are no easy answers, but the same questions must be asked and acted upon by individuals before they fight. The Vietnam War ended over 40 years ago, but these moral dilemmas are still relevant today.

LEGACY OF THE VIETNAM WAR

Whether the soldiers returning home were 'grunts' (US infantry) or the 'diggers' from Australia who had also seen service in Vietnam, their homecoming was often made difficult by the years of anti-war protests back home and by the outcome of the war. Regardless of whether any war is right or wrong, successful or not, veterans who have been sent to risk their lives in battle deserve respect, sympathy and care from society.

★ HOPE FOR THE FUTURE

Perhaps the best tribute to those from all sides who lost their lives in the Vietnam War, and later in the Afghanistan and Iraq wars, is to work for conflict resolution in the future. Politicians need to make sure that international treaty organisations such as the United Nations can act effectively and that international law is enforced and war crimes prevented. We can all work to increase international understanding in our own lives and friendships.

★ HEALING WOUNDS

Many US veterans have done remarkable work over the years, visiting Vietnam and meeting their former enemies. One veteran called Mike Boehm helped build a medical clinic and primary schools in Vietnam. He also got together with the Quang Ngai Province branch of the Vietnam Women's Union to create a Peace Park at the scene of the My Lai Massacre.

★ LEARNING THE PAST

The many Western tourists who visit Vietnam today enjoy the scenery, the beaches, the blue sea and the Mekong River. They need to read some history too, to realise that these simple pleasures are a marvel worth celebrating. World leaders and politicians also need to read their history books, if they are to learn the lessons of the Vietnam War.

"WE CANNOT FORGET THE PAST, BUT WE CANNOT LIVE WITH ANGER AND HATRED EITHER. WITH THIS PARK OF PEACE, WE HAVE CREATED A GREEN, ROLLING, LIVING MONUMENT TO PEACE."

US veteran and peace campaigner Mike Boehm.

The statue of three soldiers forms a part of the Vietnam Veterans Memorial in Washington, DC.

GLOSSARY

assassination
Murder, often for political reasons.

boat people
Refugees who flee a country in small boats.

carpet bombing
Heavy bombing on a wide scale.

casualty
Someone who is killed or injured.

ceasefire
A temporary halt to the fighting.

censorship
Official limits placed on communication.

civil rights
The rights of citizens to have the same treatment and opportunities as everyone else.

colonise
To govern or settle another country.

communism
A political system based upon pubic ownership and government by a party claiming to represent the workers.

constitution
The body of laws that defines how a nation is governed.

coup
The sudden overthrow of a government.

defoliants
Chemicals which kill vegetation.

democracy
Rule by the people or by their elected representatives.

De-Militarised Zone (DMZ)
A border strip between two warring states that armies are supposed not to enter.

détente
A relaxation of political tension.

domino theory
A theory that political change will have knock-on effect in neighbouring countries.

drones
The present-day term for unmanned aerial vehicles (UAVs), already used in the Vietnam War.

escalate
To increase or spread.

free market
Trade which has few duties and little government restraint.

guerrilla warfare
Irregular fighting, often using ambush or sabotage rather than pitched battles.

inauguration
The formal start of a new US presidency.

international law
The laws which govern relations between nations.

massacre
Killing on a large scale.

military-industrial complex
An association of arms manufacturers, governments and the military.

morale
Spirits or self-confidence.

napalm
The name given to chemicals used as incendiary weapons.

offensive
A major strategic attack across a wide area.

post-traumatic stress disorder (PTSD)
A nervous reaction to earlier stress.

puppet state
A state that is supposed to be independent, but which is dependent on another power, who 'pull its strings' like a puppet's.

ratify
To confirm a legal agreement.

spy planes
High-altitude surveillance aircraft.

stalemate
A situation where neither side in a conflict can take meaningful action.

veto
The right to reject or overturn a proposal or a vote.

FURTHER INFORMATION

★ BOOKS TO READ

Living through... The Vietnam War:
Cath Senker
(Raintree 2013)
The war and its impact, on both sides of
the conflict.

*Moments in History... Why Did the
Vietnam War Happen?:*
Clive Gifford
(Gareth Stevens 2010)
Vietnam: the causes and the controversies.

*Primary Source Detectives: Who
Protested Against the Vietnam War?*
Richard Spilsbury
(Raintree 2015)
Real stories and historical detective work.

★ MUSEUMS AND WEBSITES TO VISIT

The Vietnam Veterans Memorial, USA
Henry Bacon Drive,
Washington DC.
www.nps.gov/vive/index.htm

.
**The National Vietnam
War Museum, USA**
Weatherford,
Texas
www.nationalvnwarmuseum.org/

**The War Remnants Museum,
Vietnam**
Vo Van Tan,
Ho Chi Minh City
www.lonelyplanet.com/vietnam/ho-chi-
minh-city/sights/museums-galleries/war-
remnants-museum

**The American Air Museum
(Imperial War Museum),
UK**
Duxford,
Cambridgeshire
www.iwm.org.uk/exhibitions/iwm-duxford/
american-air-museum

www.history.com/topics/vietnam-war/
vietnam-war-history
An account of the war and the politics, with
video clips.

www.history.com/topics/vietnam-war/
vietnam-war-history
Detailed timelines and topics.

http://spartacus-educational.com/
VietnamWar.htm
Extensive coverage of the conflict and
related topics.